ALL ZARAGOZA

Text, photographs, lay-out and reproduction, entirely designed and created by the Technical Department of EDITORIAL ESCUDO DE ORO, S.A.

6th Edition

I.S.B.N. 84-378-0376-4

Dep. Legal B. 31168-1997

Editorial Escudo de Oro, S.A.

A view of the city of Saragossa, a painting by Velázquez.

THE CITY OF FOUR CULTURES

The illustrious course of the history of Saragossa is marked by the existence of four cultures, — Iberian, Roman, Arab and Christian, each of them conferring a different human and architectural aspect upon the city. Where Saragossa now stands there existed an Iberan settlement called *Salduba;* several coins have been preserved from this period with the Iberian horseman depicted on them. According to legend the settlement was founded by Tubal, the grandson of Noah, in the year 144 after the Flood.

The strategic importance of ancient *Salduba* induced the Emperor Augustus to found a military colony in the same place calling it *Caesar Augusta;* this later became the most important city in the interior of *Hispania Tarraconense.* The former city limits correspond in modern Saragossa to the space enclosed by the streets Escuelas Pías and Coso, an irregular polygon, crossed by the streets of Manifestación, Espoz and Mina, Mayor and Jaime I which comprise the old quarter of the capital of Aragón.

According to religious tradition, it was under the Roman domination in 40 A.D. when the Virgin in mortal guise, appeared on the shores of the Ebro to the Apostle James, and handed him the stone on which she had stood for it to be the future symbol of the faith of the people of Aragón.

During the period of Roman domination, Christians were fiercely persecuted in Saragossa. In the IV century Santa Engracia suffered martyrdom along with many more Christian souls. The hymns by Aurelio

Prudencio Clemente date from this period of history. After occupying an important position during the Visigothic period, Saragossa had to yield to the Arabs under the command of Muza on condition that they would respect the Christian churches already standing. The Roman city was named *Sarakosta* by the Arabs and when the Caliphate of Córdoba was dissolved in the XI century, the city played an important part when the Saragossa taifas kingdom was created.

In the year 1118, Alfonso the Battler reconquered *Sarakosta* for the Christians. The city then assumed an important historical role and became the court of the kingdom of Aragón. Its cathedral, the Seo, was built on the site of the former Moslem mosque. At the beginning of the XIV century the bishopric of Saragossa was elevated to the rank of Metropolitan, the first archbishop being the famous don Pedro de Luna. Saragossa went through a period of great splendour and the city acquired many enviable political liberties codified in the famous *Fueros* (Rights). The monarchs Ferdinand and Isabella established the court of their kingdom in Saragossa and the lovely Arab palace of la Aljafería once more became a royal seat as it had been under the Moslems.

The capital of Aragón behaved with singular heroism when Philip II annulled the Rights of Aragón and went on to impress the world with its amazing resistence against the French during the Peninsula War. Its inhabitants resisted two bloody sieges in 1808 and 1809, and, under the command of Palafox, attained the uttermost limits of bravery and heroic conduct.

The city was partially destroyed and then slowly rebuilt after the entry of the troops of Napoleon into its precincts. In the XX century Saragossa, without abandoning its agricultural and artisan tradition has become a city of considerable industrial and economic vitality being one of the most densely populated and outstanding cities in Spain.

A close-up of the monument to Augustina of Aragón.

THE EBRO; THE STONE BRIDGE AND THE BRIDGE OF SANTIAGO

The most characteristic picture there is of Saragossa is one associated with the Basilica of el Pilar and the river Ebro, the largest and most important of Spain's rivers, whose source is not far from the Cantabrian sea at Reinosa and its mouth on the Mediterranean at Amposta; on reaching the capital of Aragón standing on its right bank near to where the rivers Huerva, Gállego and Jalón flow into it, the river Ebro is at its widest. Its waters flow majestically under the bridges of Saragossa as if they wished to take a rest from their long journey and gaze in wonder at the well-known towers of el Pilar.

The outline of the Puente de Piedra (Stone Bridge) along with that of el Pilar constitutes one of the most popular and widely published views of Saragossa. The sturdy structure of the bridge — probably built on Roman foundations — includes several architectural styles. The Puente de Piedra was a stubbornly defended bastion throughout the city's history, destroyed on more than one occasion and then rebuilt, «today it stands», says Santiago Lorén, «as an almost complete synthesis of the history of Saragossa». Its ancient Roman structure was restored towards the end of the XII century.

Later when the bridge fell in, in the year 1261 after the banks of the Ebro had overflowed, the river was crossed for some time by an improvised bridge of boats. During the early parts of the XV century work was undertaken on the building of a new stone bridge which was not finished until the latter part of the century. The Stone Bridge was once more swept away in 1643 by another overflowing of the banks of the Ebro. Nearly two centuries later in 1813 the troops of Napoleon sunk it to the bottom of the river. Rebuilt yet again, the Stone Bridge has mudejar, French,

Aerial view of the Basilica of Nuestra Señora del Pilar.

The Basilica Our Lady of El Pilar. ▷

Italian and Basque architectural features. From its railings there are some attractive views of the city dominated by the Ebro and the colossal pile of the Basilica of el Pilar. Not far from the Puente de Piedra is the Santiago Bridge of graceful modern appearance from which there are also some interesting views of the city and especially of Our Lady of el Pilar, so intimately associated with the capital of Aragón.

THE BASILICA OF OUR LADY OF EL PILAR

Built to commemorate the legendary appearance of the Virgin to the Apostle James, the basilica was built to substitute the Visigothic church of Santa María la Mayor which was destroyed by fire in 1434 and from which the statue of the Virgin was miraculously saved. In the XVI century Archbishop don Hernando de Aragón ordered a large Gothic church with one nave to be built; this was pulled down a century later to make way for the construction of the present basilica of Our Lady del Pilar according to plans drawn up by Herrera el Mozo. In 1681 the first stone of the new church was laid, designed in the shape of a gigantic rectangle with three naves, chapels in the buttresses, and high towers on the four angles of the rectangle. In the XVIII century, Ventura Rodríguez built the central chapel where the statue of the Virgin del Pilar is

A close-up of the famous shrine in Our Lady of El Pilar.

The «infanticos del Pilar» rehearsing.

The popular and much worshipped statue of Our Lady of El Pilar.

An interior view of the great Saragossa church of El Pilar.

A close-up of the High-Altar in the Basilica of El Pilar.

worshipped, and changed the decoration of the basilica in accordance with neoclassical style.

The external appearance of the basilica of Our Lady of el Pilar is grandiose; particularly outstanding are the ten domes covered with coloured tiles, the enormous central dome and the four towers. The main façade is neoclassical in style and its austere tone is softened by the central altar-piece by Pablo Serrano and the large statues decorating the upper part.

The inside of the basilica is divided into three naves separated by a dozen enormous square pillars and measures 130 metres in length by 65 wide. There are several chapels situated round the pillars. The chapel of el Pilar however rises up alone in the centre of the basilica. It is neoclassical in style and has three altars, two of them decorated with sculptures by Ramírez and the third containing the statue of the Virgin which is a small gilded wooden carving in Gothic style, 38 centimetres high standing on the Sacred Column of jasper measuring two metres in height and 24 centimetres in diametre.

The high altar is worthy of mention as it is one of the few pieces that has been preserved from the old Gothic church; sculpted in alabastre by Damián Forment in the early XVI century, it is a well proportioned work of great artistic quality.

Also of interest is the vault of the choir in the Santa Capilla (Holy Chapel) painted by Goya and four vaults

Two views
of the Choir
in El Pilar.

Detail of the
magnificent
High-Altar in
Our Lady of
El Pilar.

A partial view of the impressive dome of El Pilar.

A shot of the luxurious sacristy in the church.

An impressive close-up of the dome of El Pilar painted by Goya.

painted by Bayeu, the choir, considered to be the largest in Spain, a lovely plateresque style work separated from the nave by a fine Renaissance railing made by Celma; the chapel of St. Lawrence with a painting by Ribera and a reredos by Ventura Rodríguez; the great sacristy with its collection of chalices, reliquaries, triptychs, ornaments, trays and the processional statue of the Virgin of el Pilar; the collection of Spanish and Flemish tapestries and the treasury of the Virgin's sacristy.

Two sketches of the Goya paintings decorating the dome of the Basilica of El Pilar.

LA LONJA (THE EXCHANGE)

One of the most characteristic buildings in Saragossa, la Lonja de Contratación (the Contracting Exchange) used for the business of dealing in agricultural products, especially grain, was built on the orders of Hernando de Aragón in 1541 and finished in 1551. Conceived with the idea of centralizing trade in Saragossa and to avoid dealings in public or religious places, it was one of the most important buildings of its time. Dedicated to doña Juana, don Carlos and prince Felipe, it bears the following legend on the high majestic columns outside: «This exchange is completed, may God keep it for ever, for justice, peace and good administration to reign herein; the year of our Lord 1551». The names of all the jurors of Saragossa during the period of its construction appear on a frieze. The building itself is in Renaissance style with Florentine influence, having four equal sides with three storeys, built in brick and slightly evoking the mudejar style. The first storey has large windows and elegant doors with half pointed archways; the second is like the first with circular windows inside the half pointed archways on the windows; and the third storey has a typically Aragonese gallery with archways containing other smaller arches decorated with circular medallions containing busts.

The inside of the Exchange is a square room made up of three equal sized naves with star-vaulted ceilings held up by two dozen conical pillars decorated with

An interior view of this historic building.

gilt rosettes. The front door, now closed, and the windows have plateresque style decoration on the inside. Located at the beginning of the calle de Jaime I and flanked by one of the sides of the Plaza del Pilar, the Exchange, with the monument to Goya opposite, is an outstanding example of Aragonese civic architecture.

The Exchange, with its unusual design, half Gothic and half plateresque style, adds its graceful presence to the illustrious past of the city of Saragossa. «In spite of so many changes», writes José M.ª Quadrado, — «Saragossa has preserved the elliptical shape which the Romans gave it along the river Ebro, being crossed by two streets, and looking out onto the four winds through four gates, which, now the city has grown to the west and to the south, have still remained and become famous under the name of archways.» The Exchange sets an evocative tone and is in striking contrast with the dynamic modern air of this capital city. The passing of time has in no way diminished the elegance of Saragossa's famous monuments, — La Seo, San Miguel de los Navarros, San Pablo, the Tower of Zuda, the Dean's Archway, and last but in no way least, the Exchange.

A splendid close-up of the Epiphany on the High-Altar-Piece in the Seo Cathedral at Saragossa.

A partial view of the choir in the Seo Cathedral.

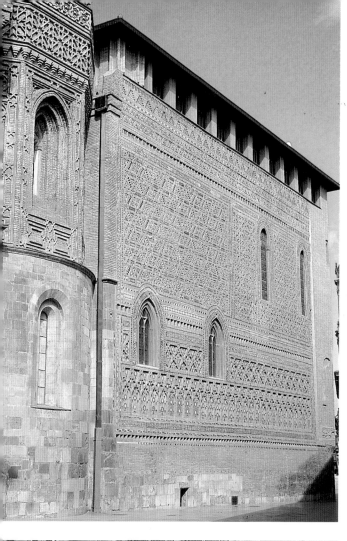

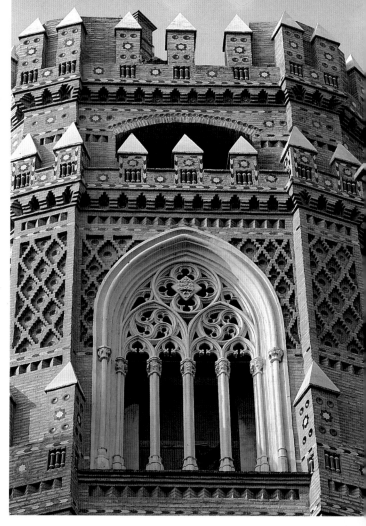

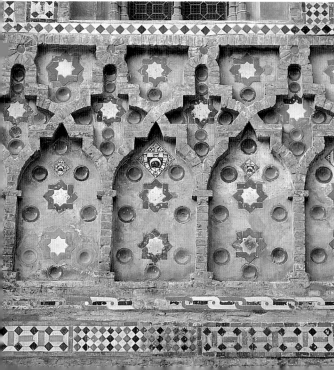

A view of
the majestic
interior of
the Seo of
Saragossa.

A fine view of the retrochoir in the Seo.

LA SEO

Built on the site of a rich Arab mosque, the cathedral of La Seo was initially a Romanesque church. After the reconquest of the city by Christian armies, the Seo of Saragossa was consecrated on January 6th 1119 in the name of the Saviour. Few remains have been preserved of the former Romanesque church, but the most valuable is the apse on the Gospel side. At the beginning of the XIV century, the building of the present cathedral was undertaken in Aragonese Gothic style and not completed until the following century. The Gothic construction substituting the Romanesque church is composed of three naves with chapels between the buttresses. The building of the church was prolonged into the XVI century and the dome was completely reconstructed, producing a fine work in mudejar style. Later, in the XVIII century the main façade was rebuilt according to neoclassical rules. The tower, dating from 1686 is the work of Juan Bautista Cartini in an accentuated Baroque style composed of four storeys and topped by a bulb-shaped capital with an elegant spire.

The façade facing the Archbishop's palace has some lovely Romanesque and Gothic windows and on the outside of the chapel known as La Parroquieta — with

A view of the cymborium in the Seo.

a Moorish-Mozarab panelled ceiling where the magnificent tomb of Lope Fernández de Luna lies with its Burgundian-Gothic style sculptures — stands a filigreed mudejar wall built in brick and decorated with multicoloured tiles with the coat of arms of the Luna family upon it. The last work carried out in the cathedral of La Seɔ was the transept portal situated on the Gospel side. it is ɔaroque in style and topped by stone sculptures depicting the Saviour, St. Peter and St. Paul.

From an architectural point of view the cathedral of La Seo is an original and harmonious construction with elements of the Romanesque, Mudejar, Gothic, Neoclassical and Baroque evident in its design. The predominating material used is brick as in the majority of the buildings in Aragón. The inside of La Seo where serveral styles are also intermingled is made up of five naves supported by some twenty solid marble columns with ogival arches. The centre of the arches is decorated with lattice work and the part before reaching the high-altar is covered by the dome built at the instigation of Benedict XIII at the beginning of the XV century.

Among the works of art in the Seo is the noteworthy reredos on the high-altar sculpted initially in alabastre by the artist Pere Johan commissioned by the archbishop don Dalmao de Mur in 1431. When he died in 1445 only a part of it had been completed, so the reredos was for the most part made by Hans Alano de Suavia. It is a truly splendid work clearly influenced by the German-Gothic style and consisting of three main sections depicting the Ascension, the Transfiguration and the Epiphany. The eucharistic monstrance in traditional Aragonese style is by Gil Morlanes.

Opposite the high-altar is the choir whose splendid stalls with their fine seating and the Papa Luna lectern were carved by the Gomar brothers in the XV century. The retrochoir is a magnificent example of Spanish Renaissance art and was carried out by several artists

The fine mudejar panelled ceiling in the Parroquieta.

A close-up of the tomb of Archbishop Lope Fernández de Luna in the Parroquieta Chapel.

in plaster, among them Arnau of Brussels and Tudelilla. Of great interest are the sculpted groups depicting the martyrdom of St. Lawrence, St. Valerus and St. Andrew. The chapels in the retrochoir are typical examples of XVII and XVIII century Aragonese carpentry. The most interesting are those of Our Lord (whose XVI century statue is much venerated in the city), the Virgin and St. John.

Other interesting chapels are: St. Michael's with a fine portal and a decorative Renaissance railing and a valuable XVI century reredos by Ancheta; St. Peter of Arbués', with its starred cross vaulting and tiled wainscoting where this saint who was killed by the Jews is buried at the foot of the high-altar and whose likeness appears below a dais held up by solomonic columns; St. Bernard's in Gothic style with a Renaissance altar-piece in alabastre and the plateresque tombs of don Hernando de Aragón and his mother; St. Mark's, with a Baroque portal in which the Monument to the Holy Sacrament in exhibited every year; St. Dominguito de Val's with its Baroque altar having a statue of Our Lady of Guadalupe of México on the upper section; St. James', in Baroque style and St. Augustin's whose altar-piece by Gil Morlanes and Gabriel Yoli is a splendid example of Aragonese Renaissance art.

In the XVIII century sacristy in the apse of the Epistle nave there are some priceless works of art to be seen which from part of the cathedral treasure. The most outstanding paintings here are, *The four Evangelists* from the XVII century Italian School, the *Glory of the Aragonese Saints,* an XVIII century work by Juan Luzán decorating the doors of the Treasure cupboard. Valuable pieces of religious metal work are kept in a cupboard with doors painted by Bayeu, and especially outstanding is the collection of busts and reliquaries donated by Papa Luna, and the busts of St. Lawrence and St. Hermenegildo. Other important pieces are the processional monstrance by Pedro Lamaisson, the

The great sacristy cupboard in the Seo.

silver chalice and liturgical robes and the fine collection of XIV, XV, XVI and XVII century Gobelins tapestries among which the most outstanding are those of *The Crucifixion, The Ships, The Wedding of Anne of Brittany* and *The coronation of the wife of Constantine.*

Other outstanding works of interest are the Gothic paintings on fabric of the XV century, — *The Preachings of St. James, the Coming and Miracles of the Virgin del Pilar.* There are also interesting collections of sketches and manuscripts preserved in La Seo.

The Seo is a particularly noteworthy building historically and architecturally and on account of its fine exterior and interior and the wealth of artistic treasure it holds, can be considered outstanding among the city's many monuments, reflecting a particularly interesting part of its past.

The magnificent bust of Saint Valerus in the church sacristy.

A close-up of the filigreed outside wall of the Parroquieta.

THE DEAN'S ARCHWAY

This is one of the loveliest and most evocative corners of Saragossa. The building dates from the XVI century and is a delightfully secluded area of the city. Deservedly, it is one of the most popular parts of Saragossa and certainly worth a visit.

THE ARAB BATHS

Situated in one of the buildings on el Coso, these baths were built in brick with stone pillars towards the end of the XIII century or at the beginning of the XIV. It is possible that they were formerly Jewish baths as they were located near to the synagogue.

SANTA MARIA MAGDALENA

A XIV century mudejar church with an elegant tower and apses in mudejar style and a Baroque portal. Of particular note inside the church are the high-altar and the altar of el Santo Cristo.

SAN MIGUEL DE LOS NAVARROS

This is a mudejar monument built in the XIV century and reconstructed in the XVI. It has a XVII century Baroque portal and an interesting high-altar piece with a statue of San Miguel de Joli by Forment.

THE CONVENT OF SANTA LUCIA

A brick building in mudejar style, this is a cloistered convent and only its fine Gothic church can be visited by the public. Of note inside this church are the original high choir.

A poetic shot of the Archway and the House of the Dean.

THE CITY

As Saragossa was, in the words of Lorén, «the multisecular roadway for all the people who have crossed the Iberian Peninsula», the city has its own peculiar appearance with the characteristic features of different civilizations. Thus, it is possible to speak of a Roman Saragossa — stretching along the streets of el Coso, Manifestación, Espoz, Mina and Mayor where the Roman Via Decumana used to be, with the still standing III century walls—; also of a mudejar Saragossa on the right bank of the Ebro, one of whose most typical buildings is «La Magdalena», a XIV century mudejar tower restored in the XVIII century, the area round La Seo and the streets leading to the calle Valenzuela, the former calle de la Morería; then there is an Arab Saragossa — *Saracosta* or *Albaida,* were the names it was given during the period of Moslem domination from which the marvellous Palace of la Aljafería and the Arab baths still remain; then, finally there is the Saragossa of the Renaissance typified by the Merchants' Exchange building, the palaces of the Morlanes and the Maestranza.

At the present time Saragossa is a developing city with an extraordinary vitality, whose main centres are the Plaza del Pilar, the Plaza de España, the Basilio Paraíso Square, and the Avenida de la Independencia. Other avenues and squares reflecting the dynamic quality of the city are: the Plaza de Aragón, with its monument to Juan Lanuza, the chief justice who defended the Rights of Aragón and faced king Philip II, the Avenues of los Pirineos, Calvo Sotelo and the Paseo de Fernando el Católico. In so far as gastronomy and night life are concerned — both very evident in the capital of Aragón — mention must be made of «el Tubo», a picturesque street with many bars and the most popular restaurants.

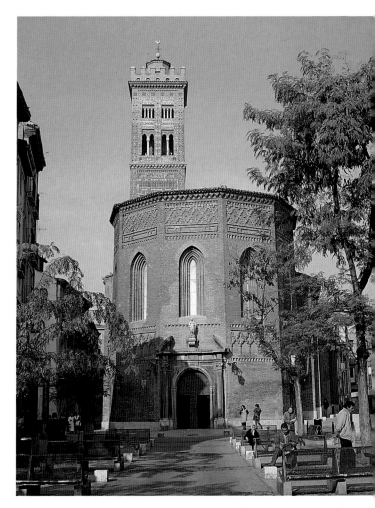

A detail from the façade of the Morlanes Palace.

A lovely close-up of the square tower on the church of San Gil Abad dating from the XIII century, and two views of the popular «el Tubo».

A view of the busy Alfonso I street. ▷

The doorway of the palace where the Law Courts of Saragossa are now housed.

THE LOCAL LAW COURTS

This building is a XVI century palace that used to belong to the family of Papa Luna and is one of the loveliest and most representative examples of Aragonese Renaissance architecture.

At the present time it is occupied by the Local Law Courts or Palace of Justice.

The front of the building is flanked by a couple of turrets and the portal with its half pointed archway is topped by a small pediment with two giant figures on either side wielding maces.

The courtyard is very large and has been restored, although its lovely Renaissance structure has been preserved. Decorated with tiles, it has a gallery which is able to be used for theatrical performances.

This ancient palace formerly belonging to the Luna family was built at the instigation of the count of Morata, and possesses the peculiarity of being one of the few buildings of its kind to have stone as an element of its construction.

THE PALACE OF THE COUNT OF ARGILLO

The present seat of the National Organization for the Blind, the palace of the Count of Argillo stands in the Plaza de San Felipe beside the church of the same name, close to the Torreón de Fortea which has now disappeared. An outstanding feature of the building is its decorative overhanging eaves carved in wood during the XVII century.

This is a typical XVII century Aragonese palace. The front is in brick with a black stone portal. The palace has a lovely courtyard and staircase of considerable proportions, together with a spherical dome.

A partial view of the lovely courtyard in the Law Courts building.

The Baroque portal of the church of San Felipe and Santiago, the façade in the same style of the church of Santa Isabel.

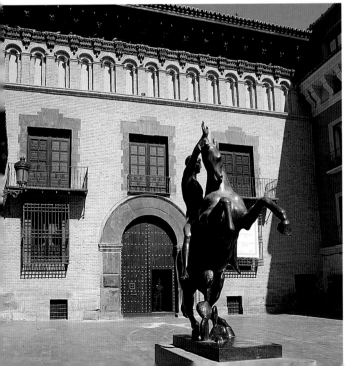

Front of the Pablo Gargallo Museum, with one of the sculptor's works in the foreground.

The Zuda Tower, next to the Church of San Juan de los Panetes.

THE ZUDA TOWER

This is a mudejar turret and the last remaining part of the former Zuda Palace built in the X century using elements and constructions of the Roman wall.

The characteristic mudejar outline of the Zuda Tower with its graceful style of architecture is situated next to the stout III century Roman walls.

THE ROMAN WALLS

These are to be found in the old part of Saragossa beside the river Ebro, at the beginning of the Av. César Augusto; there are also other parts of it near the convent of the Canonesas del Santo Sepulcro.

These Roman walls date from the II or III centuries and have circular turrets built with parallel blocks of stone.

SAN JUAN DE LOS PANETES

This church stands on the banks of the Ebro near the basilica of Our Lady of el Pilar in the centre of what was the original Iberian settlement of *Salduba.* Built in the XVIII century, the church of San Juan de los Panetes has an elegant Baroque tower in mudejar style.

SANTA ISABEL

This church, also known as San Cayetano, has a decorative Baroque façade and it is from here that the procession of the Holy Burial leaves on Good Friday; this is the climax of the Holy Week celebrations in Saragossa.

The Church of San Juan de los Panetes.

The slender tower of the church of San Pablo.

The reredos on the High-Altar by Damián Forment.

The bronze railing closing off the choir in the church of San Pablo.

SAN PABLO

Together with the Seo and the basilica del Pilar, this church makes up the trio of Saragossa's cathedrals. The church of San Pablo enjoys all the liturgical privileges of a cathedral. When it was built in the XIII century it consisted of only one nave, but later on the church was enlarged and work on this lasted until the XVIII century, San Pablo was restored in the XIV century and towards the end of the XV assumed the appearance it has today. From its original structure there remains the octagonal tower, one of the most balanced and elegant in mudejar style to be found in Aragón.

The church now has three naves and its neoclassical façade is situated in the calle San Pablo. The portal in the shape of a half pointed archway is decorated with pilastres of Tuscan shape as is the rest of the façade, and large urns decorate the niches in the intervening spaces.

Of interest inside the church is the reredos on the high altar, carved in wood by Damián Forment in the XVI century; this is one of the best works by this sculptor and one of the most representative examples of Renaissance art in Aragón, although there are some Gothic elements to be seen on the dossels. The reredos rests upon a bench decorated with six sculpted groups depicting scenes from the Passion. The Apostle Paul occupies the centre of the reredos, crowned by the monstrance of the Sagrarium.

The church choir is also of great interest; situated in the central nave between the high altar-piece and the tower, its XVI century stalls are similar to those in the Seo. The large railing closing off the choir is of bronze and was made in the XVIII century; some say it was gilded by Goya's father.

Among the chapels here, the most outstanding are, — el Pilar, with its Gothic railing and portal and plateresque style reredos; el Rosario on the Epistle side with a fine XV century reredos, and the Virgin del Populo with its Roman appellation and a XVII century Baroque reredos.

Façade of the Aljafería Palace.

THE ALJAFERIA

A pleasure palace of the Moorish kings, its construction was initiated by Aben-Alfaje in the year 864, although the most important part of the building was made by Alfufayar Almodactir in the XI century. The

Two of the filigreed Arab archways on this lovely monument.

Interior archways in the Aljafería Palace.

Panelled ceiling in the Throne Room and detail from the pillars.

A view of the mosque in the Aljafería Palace.

Aljafería palace is the most important Arab monument in Saragossa. When the city was conquered by Alfonso I, this former residence of the taifas kings of the capital of Aragón was ceded to the Benedictine order on condition that they built a church there. Throughout the XIV and XV centuries the Aljafería was inhabited by the kings of Aragón. This palace was used as a background to the work by García Gutiérrez entitled *El Trovador (Il Trovatore)* upon which the opera of the same name was inspired, with its music by Verdi and libretto by Cammarano.

In the Aljafería, whose outside belies the sumptuousness of its interior, its two different architectural stages, the Arab and the Christian, can be clearly appreciated. The Arab part of the palace constitutes an architectural link between the caliphate style of Córdoba and the Almohade of Seville. Among the Arab architectural elements the most outstanding are the St. Isabel courtyard, largely restored, where some Gothic additions can be seen, and the Oratory with its *mihrab* or prayer niche, and artistic decoration, its ceiling dating from the time of Ferdinand and Isabella. Also in Arab style is part of the Homage Tower, called the Troubador's Tower, which was originally used for defence and was where Antonio Pérez was imprisoned in Philip II's time.

Ferdinand and Isabella ordered a palace to be built on top of the Arab one, and it is from this period that most of the Christian elements preserved in the Aljafería date. The most outstanding of these elements are, the magnificent Gothic staircase with filigreed plaster bannisters leading to the royal chambers which have some fine panelled ceilings in carved wood in mudejar style; also the Sala de Santa Isabel which has some of the finest mudejar panelled ceilings in the whole of Spain; the office of don Fernando, beautifully decorated; then a room in which there is an inscription recording the birth of St. Isabel, the daughter of Pedro III of Aragón and queen of Portugal; the splendid throne room in mudejar style with a gallery held up by Gothic ornaments, and the old church with its interesting XIV century Gothic vault. The Aljafería palace was the background against which the coronation of the kings of Aragón took place, and also it was the seat of the Tribunal of the Inquisition from 1485.

Undoubtedly one of the most characteristic and popular of Saragossa's historic buildings is La Aljafería. It has an original outline and was the scene of many historic events; also, some of its chambers are still decoratively adorned and contribute to its evocative charm. Christian and Moslem elements adorn the interior and give it a specially subtle atmosphere impregnated with the aroma of the past.

Plaza de España.

The façade of the church of Santa Engracia.

THE PROVINCIAL GOVERNMENT BUILDING

This building stands in the Plaza de España and is constructed on the site of the former convent of Santo Domingo. Its façade is in neoclassical style and inside is the magnificent conference chamber, besides a collection of paintings by students and artists from the surrounding province.

SANTA ENGRACIA

This church was destroyed by the bombarding suffered by Saragossa on the night of August 13th to 14th in 1808, with the loss of the famous Gothic mudejar cloister, the library and the greater part of the building. On the present façade some mudejar elements have been preserved and the portal made by the Morlanes (father and son) is one of the most interesting and representative examples of Aragonese plateresque style.

The church crypt is also of much interest and in it there are serveral valuable paleochristian tombs.

THE CAPTAIN GENERAL'S HOUSE

A building in sober modern style, it has an elegant interior staircase leading to the private chambers and the magnificent Throne Room.

THE TOWN HALL

The new Town Hall building stands in the Plaza del Pilar and is an outstanding example of Aragonese architecture. The façade with arches and porches on both sides of the main door has two large bronze sculptures depicting St. Valerus and the Guardian Angel by the sculptor Pablo Serrano, and bears the coat of arms in stone of the city and a large clock made of wrought iron.

A sarcophagus used as an altar.

A paleochristian sarcophagus preserved in the crypt of the church of Santa Engracia.

Detail of the sculpture on the sarcophagus.

Detail from a sarcophagus used as an altar front.

City walls and the central market.

Auditorium.

A monument to Juan Lanuza in the Plaza de Aragón.

The façade of the Medical Faculty of Saragossa.

THE HOUSE OF THE DEAN

Situated in the evocative area of the Seo, and rebuilt by the Saragossa Savings-Bank, the inside of this house is especially attractive not only for its sumptuously decorated rooms but also on account of the collection of furniture and tapestries decorating it. One of the two collections of tapestries depicts a series of episodes from the book of Esther and the other from the Schönbrunn Palace in Vienna, is of mythological legends alluding to Dido and Aeneas.

THE PUERTA DEL CARMEN (THE CARMEN GATE)

This gate belonged to the ancient city walls and was built in neoclassical style towards the end of the XVIII century. Constructed in stone, it has three straight openings the lower ones being shorter.

The Carmen Gate has been declared a National Monument and it is still possible to see the traces of the destruction brought about during the long battles that took place in the famous sieges of Saragossa from 1808 to 1809.

THE UNIVERSITY

Built towards the end of the XVI century, it underwent reconstruction in the XIX century. Particularly outstanding is the large rectangular courtyard with its graceful gallery of half pointed archways, and the library containing a considerable number of volumes. At the end of the last century the spacious modern building housing the Medical Faculty was built.

A fine night time view from the central Plaza de Paraíso.

LA MAESTRANZA

The former house of don Miguel and don Lope, Renaissance in style, this building was constructed in the XVI century. Salient features of the present day Maestranza are the splendid eaves, the plateresque courtyard and the decorative mudejar panelled ceiling adorning the dome over the main staircase. A typical example of Aragonese civic architecture.

THE CHURCH OF LA MANTERIA

In former times this place of worship belonged to an Augustinian convent and is now owned by the Escolapians. Built in the XVII century, its brick façade is in Baroque style. Of much interest are the frescoes painted by Claudio Coello, assisted by Sebastián Muñoz which decorate the inside of the church.

THE CASINO

The Casino is installed in the Palace of the Count of Sástago, in the calle del Coso. Its two doors in neoclassical style are particularly fine and also the high gallery held up by graceful columns; there are also the eaves decoratively carved in wood. It houses an important library and an interesting collection of paintings.

A lovely close-up of the Puerta del Carmen.

A view of the façade of San Ildefonso.

A monument to the Sieges of Saragossa in the Plaza de los Sitios.

THE FINE ARTS MUSEUM

An impressive solid brick building in the Aragonese style, it is situated in the Plaza de los Sitios and is part of an elegant modern area occupying the site of the former orchard of Santa Engracia. The Fine Arts Museum, like the building which houses the School of Arts and Crafts, was built on the occasion of the celebration of the Universal Exhibition in 1908.

The important collections of the Archaeological Museum are housed in the Fine Arts Museum, the most valuable exhibits being iron and bronze prehistoric objects from the Aragonese resorts of Azaila, Ejea de los Caballeros, Sádaba, and Lower Aragón; pieces of Iberian pottery, Roman sculptures and mosaics, among them three exceptionally beautiful statues found in different excavations carried out in Saragossa, also the magnificent head of a woman cast in bronze — found in Fuentes de Ebro — and a sleeping faun.

Other interesting archaeological exhibits are the remains of the decoration of La Aljafería — a large frieze, capitals, sections of the schafts of columns, a mixtilinear archway and a tombstone, among others; Renaissance remains and mediaeval ones, a Gothic-mudejar arch in plaster, what remains of the magnificent Veruela stonework, several tombs and Gothic and Romanesque sculptures; artistic wrought iron work, antique weapons, carved wood and attractive tiles. Pieces of value are the so-called «Vaso Palao» from Belchite and the «terra sigillata» from Mallén.

The important Fine Arts Museum Collection is installed in several rooms distributed around an elegant plateresque style courtyard. The different periods of Spanish painting in general and Aragonese painting in particular are all represented. The room most frequently visited is the one devoted to the Aragonese painter Francisco de Goya y Lucientes, the universal

A Roman mosaic of Orpheus and the lions, *the* Virgin and Child *and a* Self-portrait *by Goya, three important works on show in the Saragossa Fine Arts Museum.*

The defence of the pulpit of San Agustín, a painting by Dumont belonging to the Fine Arts Museum.

A portrait of
Ferdinand
VII painted
by Goya.

Paseo de la Constitución.

genius in painting whose work is on show in a large luxurious room decorated with Empire style marbles and bronzes. When the museum was restored several new rooms were opened up, among them those devoted to modern painting, the Aragonese painter Marín Bagües and interesting collections of pottery, wrought iron work, coins and mediaeval remains.

Among the many fascinating works on show in the Fine Arts museum, the following are especially noteworthy — the reredos of the *Holy Sepulcher* by Serra; the reredos of the *Holy Cross of Blesa* by

Monument to the Constitución.

Plaza de San Francisco. Monument to Ferdinand the Catholic.

Miguel Jiménez and Martínez Bernat; the *Virgin with the Child and an Angel* by Huguet; the *Adoration of the Magi* by Roland de Mois; the *Virgin with the Child* by Isembrandt; the *Virgin with the Child* by Sasoferrato; *Epiphany* and a painting of *St. John the Baptist* by Cósida; *St. Joseph and the Child* by Lucas Jordán; *St. John the Evangelist* by R. Bayeu; *The Virgin and St. Thomas Aquinus* by Francisco Bayeu and other works by this same author entitled *Self-Portrait, Feliciana Bayeu* and *Merklein; Portrait of José N. Azara* by Mengs; *Don John of Austria* and *Philip II* by Pantoja; the *Blessing of Jacob* by Ribera; and *Calomarde* by Vicente López.

Goya's contribution to the Museum collection merits a description of its own; the following are the works by this artist on exhibition here: *Virgin del Pilar, Portrait of don Félix Azara, Ferdinand VII, the Duke of San Carlos* and the complete series of the *Caprices, the Disasters of War,* and *Bull-Fighting.*

The Ethnographical Section is also interesting with a fine reproduction of a *Casa Antotana* (a typical house in the Ansó region) consisting of a living room, bed room and kitchen, furnished and decorated in genuine popular style with eleven figures wearing the picturesque traditional costume of the Ansó valley.

Both the collections of paintings — among the works by Spanish artists those of Goya are particularly outstanding — and other objects decorating the rooms in the Archaeological Museum and those of the Ethnography Section make up an extremely important group of artistic works showing the great cultural potential of the capital of Aragón. The quality of these museums is part of the great artistic tradition of which Saragossa has always been proud.

Paseo Isabel La Católica.

Paseo de Pamplona.

Three beautiful views of the Avenida de San Sebastián crossing the magnificent Primo de Rivera Park.

THE SARAGOSSA PARK

A large green area in the city, for many years known as the Miguel Primo de Rivera Park, it is a real beauty spot in the city. Extremely spacious, it has gardens, ornamental pools, fountains, modern sports installations, wide avenues, attractive lanes and interesting buildings. The colossal statue of Alfonso I the Battler built on a slight rise dominates all the attractive vitality of the Saragossa Park.

The Park is reached by crossing the Plaza del Emperador Carlos along the fine bridge spanning the river Huerva, at the end of the Paseo de Fernando el Católico, and across the Avenida de San Sebastián reaching the spot where the statue stands of the Christian king who conquered *Sarakosta,* capital of the Aragonese taifal kingdom. Throughout the length and breadth of the park there are different monuments to the memory of illustrious Aragonese. The many flowers add a charming note to the park and make a pleasant contrast with the green hedges and lawns.

The children's garden with its modern amenities — two fine swimming pools and a gigantic relief map of the Iberian peninsula — augment the attractiveness of this delightful area of the city.

A close-up of the Primo de Rivera Park.

At the Park, it pervives an eternal spring, always ornamented by splendid flowers.

A partial view of the Winter Garden.

Primo de Rivera Park: monument to King Alphonse I.

The attractive Teruel-style building, housing the Natural Science Museum.

THE ETHNOLOGICAL MUSEUM

This museum is housed in a stone building typical of those built in the Pyrenees in the style characteristic of Aragonese architecture. There are some interesting ethnological collections to be seen here, among them those of typical Aragonese costumes, agricultural implements, pottery, wrought iron work, and musical in-

The Aragonese-style house where the interesting collections belonging to the Ethnological Museum are kept.

Reproduction of a typical Aragonese kitchen with models dressed in local costume, on show in the Ethnological Museum.

struments. Most attractive are the groups with scenes from High Aragón, especially those alluding to the Ansó region.

THE NATURAL SCIENCE MUSEUM

Also located in the Saragossa Park in a house near to the Ethnological Museum, whose style redolent of the province of Teruel is a faithful reproduction of a house in the Albarracín mountains — the Natural Science Museum has some good botanical, minerological and zoological collections related to the region of Aragón.

THE IMPERIAL CANAL OF ARAGON

Sited not far from Saragossa in the Torrero district, the Imperial Canal of Aragón was projected in the time of Carlos I and completed in the XVIII century by Cardinal Pignatelli. It stretches from the capital of Aragón to Tudela and is more than 100 kilometres long, 22 metres wide and nearly 3 metres deep.
It is interesting to note that on the banks of the canal in the so-called «Casa Blanca» the document of surrender of Saragossa to the French troops besieging the city was signed in 1809.

Six views of the fabulous Amusement Park in Saragossa, a real paradise for the young.

An impressive close-up of one of the parts of the famous Imperial Canal of Aragón.

The façade of the Carthusian convent of Aula Dei.

The portal of the Carthusian convent.

OUR LADY OF AULA DEI

This famous Carthusian monastery is some 10 kilometres from Saragossa on the road to Barcelona, not far from the confluence of the river Gállego with the Ebro. The construction of the church of Our Lady of Aula Dei was undertaken in the year 1564 at the instigation of don Fernando, grandson of Ferdinand and Isabella, and was rebuilt towards the end of the XVIII century and the beginning of the XIX.

The church is a solid building in brick with a finely decorated doorway. It has crossed vaulting in the galleries and cloisters and 33 chapels. The monastery has 37 cells all with a flat roof from where there are splendid views of the surrounding countryside.

The most important feature of this Carthusian monastery is the existence of some fresco paintings by Goya decorating the walls; these were done in 1772 and depict scenes from the life of the Virgin.
Of interest inside the building are — the choir and its impressive choir-stalls, the XVIII century gilt wooden reredos, the library whose valuable content came from the French monasteries of Valbonne and Vauclair, the Holy Shrine with some priceless relics, the spacious refectory and monks' kitchen.

The magnificent choir-stalls in the Carthusian convent of
Aula Dei. ▷

◁ *Three details from the decorative artisanry in Aula Dei.*

Three paintings showing the quality of the pictures to be found in the Carthusian convent of Our Lady of Aula Dei.

Four views of the popular processions of giants and large-headed figures («cabezudos») going through the streets in celebration of the festivities of el Pilar.

Couples dressed in typical Aragonese costume dancing the «Jota», one of Spain's most popular dances.

Groups of young people in regional costume ready to take part in a folklore festival.

FOLKLORE

Saragossa is the capital of one of the regions with the richest and most varied folklore in the whole of Spain. There are many traditions and extremely varied popular customs that are still preserved in Saragossa. The popular costume of Saragossa is distinguished by its sober elegance. With a few variations it is the one generally worn in Lower Aragón, that is, «el Baturro». The man wears knee breeches made of corduroy or velvet, slashed at both sides allowing the white under trouser to be seen, white, blue or black stockings, sandals made from hemp with black laces, a purple or red sash to hold up the breeches wound three times round the waist, a white shirt, velvet waistcoat adorned on feast days with embroidery, jet or glass beads, and on the head the typical «cachirulo» usually a silk handkerchief with black and red squares is worn.

The lady wears a full skirt made of percale in a branched design, a bodice with long sleeves in the same material, a Manila type shawl in fine silk or simple cloth folded into two with the point at the back, white stockings, rope-soled sandals with black laces often substituted on festive occasions by low-heeled black shoes with a buckle or bow. The lady in the popular costume of Saragossa wears the «bancal» made of black velvet and decorated with beading, with this she covers her head and part of her face for religious ceremonies.

The *jota* is the dance and popular song par excellence not only in Saragossa but the whole of Aragón. There is an Official School of the Aragonese Jota in Saragossa connected to the Conservatory of Music. The *jota* is a song and dance that is full of dynamism and feeling, gay and poetical, closely linked to folklore of Arab origin, according to those who have studied the subject. It is usually sung with an accompaniment of guitars, bandurrias, and tambourines with other musical instruments sometimes taking part, usually guitars and lutes. The *jota* is danced in pairs.

Three views of the brilliant solemnity characterising the processions in Saragossa.

Among the different varieties of the *jota* danced in this region, the Saragossa version is the most graceful and representative. Danced in the whole province, the *jota* is also an item in any folklore festival either in Spain or abroad, and many are the occasions when it is danced spontaneously by the townspeople.

The Fiesta Mayor (Annual Celebration) in the city of Saragossa is especially noteworthy and has been declared of «Tourist Interest»; celebrated on October 12th the day of el Pilar, it has a procession of giants and large headed figures *(cabezudos),* an offering of flowers from all Spain to the Virgin, and the spectacular Rosary of Crystal; the festivities of St. Valerus on January 29th and the spring celebrations with theatrical and operatic performances and the celebration of the International Fair of Agricultural Machinery are outstanding too. Also of note is the National Samples Fair held in October.

An attractive night time shot with the Basilica of El Pilar reflected in the waters of the Ebro.

A view of the outside of the Bull-ring at Saragossa.

ARTS AND CRAFTS

Thanks to the efforts of various groups and its own «Craft Law», Aragon has kept its craft heritage very much alive. Amongst the different crafts in existence, ceramic art is, without doubt, the most common. Besides pottery, decorated ceramic work is also to be found, having been introduced by the Moors. The most characteristic such pieces are adorned with Mudéjar motifs (floral patterns and geometric forms), typically in such colours as dark green and violet, as the colours are generally made from copper and cobalt oxides. Zaragoza Fair, held in December, is the ideal place to see and buy craftwork from Aragon, including, as well as ceramics, wrought-iron work articles made from linen, hemp and wool.

GASTRONOMY

Exalted by travellers and in works of literature, the *cuisine* of Aragon and, therefore, of Zaragoza, is rich and varied. The basic ingredients are fresh-grown fruit and vegetables, different types of meat, and fish. The most typical local dishes include chicken or rabbit «a la chilindrón», a tasty condiment made from tomato, pimento, onion, garlic, oil and pepper; «ajoarriero» cod, made with potatoes, onion, garlic, eggs and garlic mayonnaise; «huevos al salmorejo», eggs heated in an earthenware dish with pork loin, *longaniza* pork sausage and asparagus; and *ternasco asado* (roast lamb). As for and wine, the reds of Cariñena and Campo de Borja are rightly famed. These wine-growing regions, with Denomination of Origin, now also produce white wines and even *cava,* champagne. The star turn in the desserts of Aragon, which include numerous local delicacies, is «guirlache», a kind of *turrón* or nougat, made with burnt sugar, almonds and adorned with hundreds and thousands.

A general view of the La Romareda Footbaall Field.

Chicken «a la chilindrón».

The slender mudejar tower of the church of Santa María de Utebo (XVI century).

UTEBO

A village situated some 12 kilometres from Saragossa, its mudejar style church of Santa María is of interest, having one nave; this church was reconstructed in the XVI century and declared a National Monument. Its slender tower — reproduced in the «Spanish Village» of the Barcelona Universal Exhibition — is built with bricks and tiles and is one of the loveliest and most representative examples of Aragonese mudejar architecture.

EJEA DE LOS CABALLEROS

The capital of the so-called five towns, the other four being Tauste, Sádaba, Sos del Rey Católico and Uncastillo, Ejea de los Caballeros has lately become a town of considerable industrial and economic development. The modernization of its irrigation system and the installation of centres for the industrialization of agricultural products in the area have motivated the construction of many buildings which has enlarged this progressive town considerably. On the other hand, new irrigation villages have grown up, among these the most outstanding are Santa Anastasia and El Bayo, which have increased the rural area surrounding Ejea de los Caballeros. Nevertheless, the markedly Aragonese character of the town has been preserved especially in the town centre of Ejea, with the church of El Salvador, an original fortress-church, half crenelated castle, half Gothic church dominating the scene. Built in the XIII century it has a solidly elegant barbican tower flanked by four tabernacles. Inside there are some decorative Renaissance altar-pieces.

Also of interest are: the mudejar church of Santa María, the walls, the convent of San Francisco where parliement met with king Jaime I present, the castle of Sora, and the hermitage of la Oliva.

The beautiful church of the Saviour at Ejea de los Caballeros, a XIII century Romanesque monument.

UNCASTILLO

An exceptionally rich town historically, Uncastillo, viewed from the cliff of Ayllón, a magnificent natural platform on the castle, is a delightful sight.

Outstanding among the historical buildings at Uncastillo are the Roman ruins of los Bañales, the decorative XII century Romanesque doorway of the chuch of Santa María and the Romanesque remains of the church of San Juan. Both these churches have been declared National Monuments. Of much interest too is the XIII-XIV century castle cum citadel and the Renaissance Town Hall building.

Overall view of Uncastillo.

SOS DEL REY CATOLICO

The birthplace of Ferdinand of Aragón, Sos del Rey Católico is an essentially mediaeval town and one of the most interesting of Aragon's towns historically. The buildings of most note in Sos del Rey Católico are: the palace of the Sada where Ferdinand of Aragón was born, inside which there is a lovely XIII century Gothic oratory, the XVI century Town Hall building, the elegant house of Luis Santangel, the XIV century Carmelite convent, the walls, the castle and the Romanesque church of San Esteban from whose tower there is a fine view of the town.

TARAZONA

Sited on the banks of the river Queiles, on mountainous land that reaches the foot of Moncayo, Tarazona, officially known as «the mudejar city», is considered to be the Toledo of Aragón on account of the quantity and value of its monuments.

Tarazona's most outstanding monument is its cathedral. Built in the XIII century it has three naves with an apse-aisle, a Gothic-mudejar tower and a Gothic cloister with mudejar screens.

Other monuments of undoubted interest are the church of the Magdalena, originally Romanesque in

Overall view Sos del Rey Católico.

The Descent from the
Cross, *a valuable
painting kept in the
cathedral at Tarazona.*

The Presentation,
*another of the
paintings belonging to
the collection of works
of art in the cathedral.*

The stone cross in front of which the poet Bécquer used to sit, and two views of the Monastery of Santa María de Veruela.

structure, restored in Renaissance style in the XVI century with a fine mudejar tower; the church of San Francisco in whose chapel of La Piedad Cisneros was made Archbishop of Toledo; the church of San Atilano — built in the XVIII century in the same place in which the house had stood where the saint was born; the Episcopal Palace, constructed on the site of an old Arab palace; the Archway of Treason, and the Cristo Bridge.

An elegant Romanesque portal leading to the church of Santa María de Veruela.

This room was kept as a Scriptorium *or copying room for the monks at Veruela.*

THE MONASTERY OF SANTA MARIA DE VERUELA

This fine monument is situated at the foot of Moncayo in the municipality of Vera del Moncayo amid scenery of tranquil beauty. On the site of the Monastery of Santa María de Veruela once stood the Iberian village of La Oruña where the iron mined in el Moncayo was worked with exceptional artistry. This famous monastery is 13 kilometres from Tarazona and 86 from Saragossa and is reached by a small road some 10 kilometres from Borja, the former Iberian *Bursao,* a picturesque village in attractive Moorish style. The view to be seen here is truly delightful with the stern majestic Moncayo mountains in the background.

The Monastery of Veruela, formerly of the Cistercian order and now staffed by the Jesuit fathers, was founded in the XII century by Pedro de Atarés. Originally inhabited by French monks it is undoubtedly one of the finest and most important monuments in the large and varied region of Moncayo.

Santa María de Veruela is completely surrounded by a solid crenelated wall with circular turrets giving it a characteristic air. The church in the monastery is of stone and reminds us in its style of the Monastery of Poblet in the province of Tarragona which also belonged to the Cistercian order. Its portal is

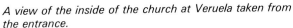
A view of the inside of the church at Veruela taken from the entrance.

The much venerated statue of Our Lady of Veruela.

Romanesque and sober in style decorated with elaborate towers.

The inside consists of three spacious solemn naves in which it is easy to detect the architectural transition from the Romanesque to the Gothic. This tendency is even more evident in the refectory which has the typical Gothic cross-vaulting in the Chapter House and in the exquisitely evocative cloister. However the elegant high gallery clearly belongs to the plateresque style.

Inside the Monastery of Veruela there are some interesting Byzantine chapels, a Byzantine kitchen, a Baroque sacristy, the old library and monks' dormitory, later known as the Salón de los Reyes.

On the outside, apart from the walls and the impressive square turret — built in the XII and XIII centuries, mention must be made of the Abbot's palace dating from the XVI century.

The stone cross is still standing on whose stone steps the poet Gustavo Adolfo Bécquer used to sit during his stay at the monastery of Veruela. The monastery accumulated some valuable art treasures many of which are now part of the patrimony of the nearby village of Vera, among them the decorative high altar of the church. Others belong to the Saragossa Museum and the Provincial Museum in Saragossa.

This monastery is closely linked to the memory of Bécquer. This Spanish Romantic poet spent some

*Six details from
the fine dossels
in the cloister,
the Gothic
cloister and
Miserere portal,
and the
Baroque
entrance to the
sacristy of
Santa María de
Veruela.*

time in a monk's cell in the monastery in an effort to cure the tuberculosis which was to cause his death at an early age. This great lyric poet from Seville wrote his famous «Legends» and some of his lovely «Rhymes» in Veruela. Gustavo Adolfo Bécquer was delighted with the virile landscape of Moncayo and explored the whole region describing in his letters the charming little picturesque villages scattered in the valleys or perched on steep cliffs. From Veruela it is easy to reach the attractive mountain peaks which serve as a backdrop to the Moncayo region and the enchanting area of Somontano where the Sanctuary of La Misericordia stands, — an impressive mountain summer resort; also Bulbuente, Ambel and Borja, villages whose churches contain altar-pieces and religious objects in precious metal of great value.

An allegory sculpted on the tomb of Abbot Lupo in the Monastery of Veruela.

A partial view of Calatayud, the second most important city in the province of Saragossa.

CALATAYUD

This city stands on flat land between the spurs of two hills on the banks of the Jalón at its confluence with the river Jiloca. After Saragossa, Catalayud is the most important city in the province and the second centre for communication in all Aragón. The birthplace of the poet Martial, it was a city of much importance during the Roman occupation, at which time it enjoyed the privilege of minting money.

A few kilometres from Calatayud are the remains of the Roman city of *Bilbilis.* Remains of the past greatness of Calatayud are to be found in the Bámbola mountains, near to the town of that name. Its name, *Kalat-Ayub* (Moorish king) was given to it by the Arabs when they settled on the site of the Iberian town of *Bámbola* and the Roman *Bilbilis.*

The city of Calatayud has two clearly marked areas, — the picturesque upper part called the Morería, topped with mudejar towers, and then the lower part of modern design.

Among its many outstanding monuments is the Collegiate Church of Santa María consecrated in the XIII century, built in mudejar style and later reconstructed. It stands in the square of the same name and has a fine plateresque portal, exquisitely worked in alabastre and an elegant octagonal mudejar tower.

The leaning tower of San Pedro de los Francos, the churches of the Holy Sepulchre and San Francisco, the Casino Principal — Barón de Warsage's former palace — the Town Hall, the Arab castle of Doña Martina and the palaces of the Heredias, García de la Vega, Esparza and Muñones are all of exceptional local and historical interest.

The Plateresque portal of the Collegiate church of Santa María.

The Homage Tower on the ancient Monastery at Piedra.

THE MONASTERY AT PIEDRA

Situated on the banks of the Piedra river in the municipality of Nuévalos, the monastery was founded in the XII century by the Cistercian monks of Poblet and restored in the XIX century. The gateway in the wall belonging to the old monastery is still preserved along with the majestic staircase with its ogival vault, the Homage Tower, and a church in Romanesque-Gothic transitional style, the cloister in ogival style, the cells with their ogival and mudejar windows, the chapter house, kitchen and spacious refectory. The remains of the monastery together with the grottos,

The apse of the old church of the Monastery at Piedra.

A delightful close-up of the lovely «Ash tree cascade» in the natural park of the Monastery at Piedra.

A poetic shot of the «Lake of Mirrors».

The «Rainbow Waterfall», another of the astonishing examples of natural beauty to be found in the park.

A striking shot of the «Trinity Waterfall».

gardens, water falls, lakes and exuberant vegetation make up the National Park of the Monastery at Piedra, declared a National Picturesque Spot, and described thus in the words of the poet don Ramón de Campoamor, — «if art is the eighth wonder of the world, natural art is the first».

The prettiest parts of the National Park of the Monastery at Piedra, whose monastery and surrounding lands were bought in 1840 by Pablo Muntadas whose son Juan Federico converted it into what it is today, are the lakes of «los Patos» (the ducks) and «El Espejo (the mirror), the latter name given by the poet Maragall—, also the fantastic «horse's tail» waterfall, an enormous grotto reached by a tunnel dug out of the living rock in 1860 at the instigation of Juan

Federico Muntadas, — the cascades known as the «Bath of Diana» and the «Ash-tree», the «Lonely one» the «Caprice», the «Devil's cliff», «the Bacchante», «the Artist» and «the Panther».

At every instant one comes upon fantasies of Nature in truly prodigious forms: steps cut out of the rock, bridges hanging over precipices with roaring foaming water beneath and glistening stones. The acrobatics of the water continuously tracing fine filigree work in the air and on the stones combine with the delightfully magical presence of a magnificent wood made up of aspens, chestnut trees, ash trees, walnut, willow and lindens giving this enchanting spot a delightful freshness in marked contrast to the arid countryside around the National Park of the Monastery at Piedra.

«The Waders», «Artist's Grotto», «Panther's Grotto» and the «Horse's Tail» waterfall, four spots of particular interest in the Monastery at Piedra.

«Diana's Bath» and the «Caprice» waterfall.

A general view of Daroca.

Puerta Alta, a popular monument in this walled town.

Puerta Baja, another interesting monument in Daroca.

The road leading to this beautiful fortified town.

DAROCA

A town of ancient origins situated in a declivity and surrounded by a lovely verdant plain, Daroca is now an agricultural centre of some importance. At a height of 753 metres above sea level, the town is an evocative picturesque sight. It is one of the oldest towns in Aragón and on more than one occasion the seat of parliaments summoned by the kings of Aragón.

The walls surrounding the town's perimeter for more than three kilometres are in a very good state of preservation and are fortified by many towers, some of which have a peculiar and interesting history, like the so-called White Eagle tower, or the Knight of the Spur, Braggart or St. George's tower or the Zoma, a Moorish tower built by the Agarenes. The walled precinct of Daroca is an impressive sight with its battlements and loopholes revealing its dynamic role in mediaeval times.

«The town», writes Santiago Lorén, «was formerly isolated when night fell and the two gates at either end of the calle Mayor were closed: la Alta or the Saragossa gate of modest design but attractive in appearance, and la Baja a fine example of the military type of architecture of the time of Charles I whose imperial coat of arms hangs above the archway».

Another outstanding building in Daroca is the Gothic parish church accupying the central apse of a former Romanesque church from which several valuable paintings have been preserved. This church, dating from the time of Juan II of Aragón was restored during the reign of Ferdinand and Isabella. Inside there are some excellent sculptures and bas-reliefs.

The original fountain with twenty spouts, a monument in Daroca dating from the XVII century.

The lovely Plaza del Generalísimo at Daroca.

The Chapel of the Sagrados Corporales *in XV century Burgundian-Gothic style.*

A close-up of the Sagrados Corporales *(XV century).*

The chapel of the Sagrados Corporales has a Gothic work with three pointed archways and walls with reliefs depicting the Birth of Christ. The XV century alabastre reredos was apparently donated by Juan II and made by Juan de la Huerta.

In this chapel we can see the imprint of the Holy Blood which, according to religious tradition was left by six Sacred Hosts taken by six Christian captains

about to take part in the defense of a position under attack by the Arabs.

The church has an important Parish Museum which preserves, along with other pieces of outstanding value, — a monstrance-reliquary in gilded silver by Pedro Moragues in 1384; fragments of a XV century alabastre reredos and some tablets by Bartolomé Bermejo.

Also of interest is the church of Santo Domingo with one XII century Romanesque section and another in Gothic and mudejar style belonging to the XIII century, also the old church of San Miguel, which although Romanesque has many Baroque additions, then there is «La Mina», a XVI century covered gallery to give outlets to the waters.

The façade of the parish church at Daroca.

The interior of the Basilica at Daroca.

A XVI century organ and XV century choir-stalls in the Basilica of Daroca.

A Gothic reredos dating from the XIII century.

Another fine Gothic reredos.

The apse and portal of the Romanesque church of San Miguel de Daroca.

CARIÑENA

Capital of the agricultural region of Cariñena, justly famed for its excellent wines, Cariñena is situated on the banks of the Jalón. It has several noteworthy buildings, the most outstanding of these being the parish church, a solid construction that used to be a fortress of the Knights of St. John, having an original crenelated octagonal tower; and the Town Hall in Aragonese style elegant lattice work.

FUENDETODOS

The native village of the painter of genius don Francisco de Goya y Lucientes, Fuendetodos is a small place some 44 km. from Saragossa, close to Herrera de los Navarros, a picturesque little Moorish village, whose main tourist attraction is a visit to the house cum museum of the painter of *The Naked Maja.* It is a humble dwelling, sparsely furnished with a plaque on the outside commemorating Goya's birth.
There is a monument to the great painter beside the church of Fuendetodos by the sculptor Julio Antonio.

CASPE

Formerly belonging to the Knights of St. John, it was here in Caspe where the comissioners who chose Ferdinand of Antequera to be king of Aragón met together in the year 1412. Caspe is the centre of a region that played an important part in prehistoric times — there were several settlements here in the first and second Iton Age — and also in the Roman period. Now it is a lovely mediaeval town with irregular winding streets, mostly in the evocative Muela district, and houses of ancient lineage.
Among the town's most important monuments are

Cariñena: Town Hall.

The kitchen in the house at Fuendetodos where Goya was born.

Part of the house where Goya was born.

the Collegiate church of Santa María la Mayor where the famous *Compromise* bearing the name of the locality was signed in 1412. There is an interesting Roman tomb in the gardens of the church. Its portal is Gothic and in the interior are XIII century Romanesque remains and some XIV century Gothic ones. Santa María la Mayor was enlarged in the XVI century. Its chapel of the Vera Cruz and the chalice of the *Compromise* are of historical interest. Also noteworthy are the ruins of a Roman temple, apparently dating from the last years of the Empire, and the Iberian foundations of La Tallada and Palermo situated within the municipality of Caspe.

A view of the Collegiate church of Caspe.

A charming dawn study of Saragossa.

EPILOGUE

Saragossa and its province, besides offering us a lesson in history, gives us a surprisingly agreable glimpse of its varied architecture and equally varied countryside.

All types of art and scenery are to be found here making an ideal crossroads of styles and landscapes. The capital gives us rich artistic and historical gifts from the past, and other towns in the province are justly famed too for their history, their wealth of monuments and for the beauty of the scenery surrounding them.

Throughout the land of Saragossa the visitor is constantly surprised and full of admiration at seeing so many works of art and so much natural beauty.

The Monastery at Piedra amazes us with the extraordinary variety of natural charms surrounding the remains of this ancient Cistercian monastery; the Monastery at Veruela with «the long series of ogives, festooned with clover leaves, among them a dumb and horrible face, these thousands of fantastic and capricious creations of the imagination that the mysterious art of the Middle Ages left carved in the granite of its basilicas» reminds us as it did Bécquer of the poetry of time past. If history and art have been generous with the province of Saragossa, culture, traditions and customs have also left their mark on the soul of the people of this region, giving them a generous and welcoming nature with two salient human characteristics — hospitality and cheerfulness.

Contents

Collection ALL EUROPE

#		Spanish	French	English	German	Italian	Catalan	Dutch	Swedish	Portuguese	Japanese	Finnish
1	ANDORRA	•	•	•	•	•	•	•				
2	LISBON	•	•	•	•	•	•			•		
3	LONDON	•	•	•	•	•	•				•	
4	BRUGES	•	•	•	•	•		•				
5	PARIS	•	•	•	•	•					•	
6	MONACO	•	•	•	•	•						
7	VIENNA	•	•	•	•	•						
11	VERDUN	•	•	•	•	•		•				
12	THE TOWER OF LONDON	•	•	•	•							
13	ANTWERP	•	•	•	•	•		•				
14	WESTMINSTER ABBEY	•	•	•	•	•						
15	THE SPANISH RIDING SCHOOL IN VIENNA	•	•	•	•	•						
16	FATIMA	•	•	•	•	•				•		
17	WINDSOR CASTLE	•	•	•	•	•					•	
19	COTE D'AZUR	•	•	•	•	•						
22	BRUSSELS	•	•	•	•	•		•				
23	SCHÖNBRUNN PALACE	•	•	•	•	•		•				
24	ROUTE OF PORT WINE	•	•	•	•	•				•		
26	HOFBURG PALACE	•	•	•	•	•						
27	ALSACE	•	•	•	•	•		•				
31	MALTA				•	•	•					
32	PERPIGNAN	•										
33	STRASBOURG	•	•	•	•	•						
34	MADEIRA + PORTO SANTO		•	•	•					•		
35	CERDAGNE - CAPCIR		•				•					
36	BERLIN	•	•	•	•	•						

Collection ART IN SPAIN

#		Spanish	French	English	German	Italian	Catalan	Dutch	Swedish	Portuguese	Japanese	Finnish
1	PALAU DE LA MUSICA CATALANA	•		•			•					
2	GAUDI	•	•	•	•	•					•	
3	PRADO MUSEUM I (Spanish Painting)	•	•	•	•	•					•	
4	PRADO MUSEUM II (Foreign Painting)	•	•	•	•	•						
5	MONASTERY OF GUADALUPE	•										
6	THE CASTLE OF XAVIER	•	•	•	•						•	
7	THE FINE ARTS MUSEUM OF SEVILLE	•	•	•	•	•						
8	SPANISH CASTLES	•	•	•	•							
9	THE CATHEDRALS OF SPAIN	•	•	•	•							
10	THE CATHEDRAL OF GERONA	•	•	•	•							
14	PICASSO	•	•	•	•	•					•	
15	REALES ALCAZARES (ROYAL PALACE OF SEVILLE)	•	•	•	•	•						
16	MADRID'S ROYAL PALACE	•	•	•	•	•						
17	ROYAL MONASTERY OF EL ESCORIAL	•	•	•	•	•						
18	THE WINES OF CATALONIA	•										
19	THE ALHAMBRA AND THE GENERALIFE	•	•	•	•	•						
20	GRANADA AND THE ALHAMBRA	•										
21	ROYAL ESTATE OF ARANJUEZ	•	•	•	•	•						
22	ROYAL ESTATE OF EL PARDO	•	•	•	•	•						
23	ROYAL HOUSES	•	•	•	•	•						
24	ROYAL PALACE OF SAN ILDEFONSO	•	•	•	•	•						
25	HOLY CROSS OF THE VALLE DE LOS CAIDOS	•	•	•	•	•						
26	OUR LADY OF THE PILLAR OF SARAGOSSA	•	•	•	•		•					
27	TEMPLE DE LA SAGRADA FAMILIA	•	•	•	•	•	•					
28	POBLET ABTEI	•	•	•	•		•					

Collection ALL SPAIN

#		Spanish	French	English	German	Italian	Catalan	Dutch	Swedish	Portuguese	Japanese	Finnish
1	ALL MADRID	•	•	•	•	•					•	
2	ALL BARCELONA	•	•	•	•	•	•				•	
3	ALL SEVILLE	•	•	•	•	•					•	
4	ALL MAJORCA	•	•	•	•	•						
5	ALL THE COSTA BRAVA	•	•	•	•	•						
6	ALL MALAGA and the Costa del Sol	•	•	•	•	•			•			
7	ALL THE CANARY ISLANDS (Gran Canaria)	•	•	•	•	•			•	•		
8	ALL CORDOBA	•	•	•	•	•					•	
9	ALL GRANADA	•	•	•	•	•			•		•	
10	ALL VALENCIA	•	•	•	•	•						
11	ALL TOLEDO	•	•	•	•	•					•	
12	ALL SANTIAGO	•	•	•	•	•						
13	ALL IBIZA and Formentera	•	•	•	•	•						
14	ALL CADIZ and the Costa de la Luz	•	•	•	•	•						
15	ALL MONTSERRAT	•	•	•	•	•	•					
16	ALL SANTANDER and Cantabria	•		•								
17	ALL THE CANARY ISLANDS II, (Tenerife)	•	•	•	•	•						•
20	ALL BURGOS	•	•	•	•	•						
21	ALL ALICANTE and the Costa Blanca	•	•	•	•	•		•				
22	ALL NAVARRA	•	•	•	•							
23	ALL LERIDA	•	•	•	•		•					
24	ALL SEGOVIA	•	•	•	•	•						
25	ALL SARAGOSSA	•	•	•	•	•			•			
26	ALL SALAMANCA	•	•	•	•	•						
27	ALL AVILA	•	•	•	•	•						
28	ALL MINORCA	•	•	•	•	•						
29	ALL SAN SEBASTIAN and Guipúzcoa	•										
30	ALL ASTURIAS	•		•								
31	ALL LA CORUNNA and the Rías Altas	•	•	•	•							
32	ALL TARRAGONA	•	•	•	•	•						
33	ALL MURCIA	•	•	•	•							
34	ALL VALLADOLID	•	•	•	•							
35	ALL GIRONA	•	•	•	•							
36	ALL HUESCA	•	•									
37	ALL JAEN	•	•	•	•							
38	ALL ALMERIA	•	•	•	•							
40	ALL CUENCA	•	•	•	•							
41	ALL LEON	•	•	•	•							
42	ALL PONTEVEDRA, VIGO and the Rías Bajas	•	•	•	•							
43	ALL RONDA	•	•	•	•	•						
44	ALL SORIA	•										
46	ALL EXTREMADURA	•	•	•	•	•						
47	ALL ANDALUSIA	•	•	•	•	•						
52	ALL MORELLA	•	•	•	•		•					

Collection ALL AMERICA

#		Spanish	French	English	German	Italian	Catalan	Dutch	Swedish	Portuguese	Japanese	Finnish
1	PUERTO RICO	•		•								
2	SANTO DOMINGO	•		•								
3	QUEBEC			•	•							
4	COSTA RICA	•		•								
5	CARACAS	•		•								

Collection ALL AFRICA

#		Spanish	French	English	German	Italian	Catalan	Dutch	Swedish	Portuguese	Japanese	Finnish
1	MOROCCO	•	•	•	•	•						
2	THE SOUTH OF MOROCCO	•	•	•	•	•						
3	TUNISIA		•	•	•	•						
4	RWANDA		•									

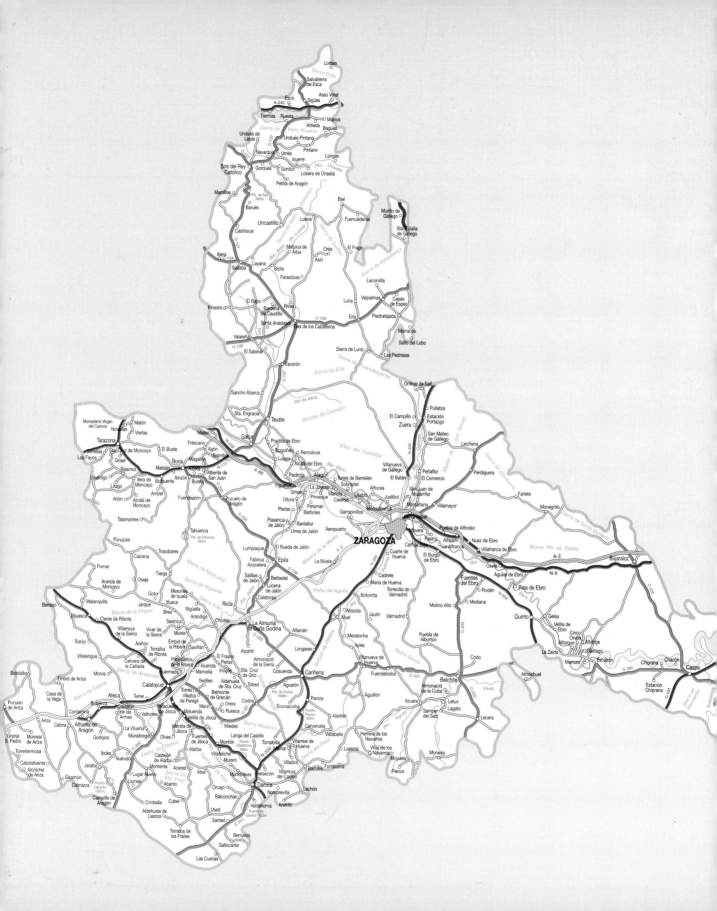